The Magic of Music

How To Attract
Your Heart's Desire
Even If You Can't Sing!

*This Book Was Made Possible
Due To A Generous Grant
From The Creative Source*

First Edition: September 2014
Second Edition: June 2017

Published by: Snowbird Books

Editor: Austin Partridge
Book Designer: Creative Culture
Cover Graphics: Apple Garageband Contents

Author Photo: Eye of The Mind Photography

Library and Archives Canada Cataloguing in Publication

Delorie, Oliver Luke, 1975-, author
    The magic of music : how to attract your heart's desire, even if you can't sing / Oliver Luke Delorie.

ISBN 978-0-9735918-6-6 (pbk.)

    1. Music--Psychological aspects. 2. Psychoanalysis and music. 3. Music therapy. 4. Visualization. I. Title.

ML3830.D45 2014   781.1'1   C2014-901499-6

Email the author at: oliverlukedelorie@gmail.com
Find more books at: SnowbirdBooks.com

P.S. This stuff changes lives. Please enjoy responsibly ☺

TABLE OF CONTENTS

Music is the strongest
form of magic.

Marilyn Manson

FOREWORD

What do music and science have in common? The cheat sheet answer can be found in the Hindu Sam Veda, the earliest known human literature on music. Music as a science, the Sam Veda tells us, is based on the continual moving and working of the planets, the vibrational sounds of the cosmos.

Music, musicians, and singers in Vedic times were eons ahead of our twenty-first century scientists as far as the influence of the planets on Earth and especially where we earthlings are concerned. Quite possibly, it is the music of the spheres that birthed science, philosophy, existentialism, poetry, dance, metaphysics, mysticism, social and cultural revolutions.

Cosmic vibrational sounds led not only to the human voice breaking into song, they inspired the creation of musical instruments that would echo their primordial rhythms and harmonies.

The musicians and singers of antiquity had the freedom, the full liberty to express without the restrictions of the Top Ten lists, music awards or groupies, much like we find and love in the music of today's indigenous peoples.

Heaven's kiss of inspiration was upon their music and song that brought down the rain upon droughts, healed the sick, safely navigated hunters through poisonous terrains, and bestowed mystical visions upon shamans.

"The yogis regulated the rhythm of the circulation, of the heart and of every action of the breath with the help of the vibration of music in tone and rhythm," wrote the Sufi master and musician Hazrat Inayat Khan, illustrating the impact of music upon body, mind, and spirit.

Everything in the
universe has a rhythm;
everything dances.

Maya Angelou

It is interesting to note that when we are seeking to solve a problem, capture or recapture a thought or an idea, we unconsciously begin to tap our fingers on a table, or maybe we begin to pace back and forth, or turn round and round like a whirling dervish.

Perhaps our method is the opposite and we use a yogic breath meditation and attune to the profound sound of silence. Application of any of these methods shifts our normal breathing pattern uniting cadence, rhythm and sound in such a way that presto! the manifestation of the desired solution or idea intuitively appears.

The human voice also is a vibrational vehicle that not only reveals much about the singer or speaker, but also has an effect upon its listeners.

Whether in a group or one-on-one intimate conversation, your voice attracts people into your magnetic field or repels them from it. Voice carries the elements of nature - earth, water, fire, air and ether. Every word vibrates according to the spirit you put into it, and consulting your voice has the power to reveal much about yourself.

Oliver Luke Delorie and *The Magic of Music* are trustworthy friends, tenderly taking you by the hand and introducing you to the far-reaching effects of the vibrational power of music to manifest pure magic in your life.

Read it once and you will be awed. Read it twice and you will be magnetized. Practice its universal principles and you will be transformed.

Michael Bernard Beckwith
Founder and Spiritual Director
Agape International Spiritual Center

"Mom, when I grow up
I'd like to be a musician."
~
"You know honey,
you can't do both."

INTRODUCTION

Busking on street corners in other countries, promoting all-age gigs in various communites, and holing up in basement bedrooms like a mad scientist led to this book, my attempt to impress upon you how enjoyable (and easy) it can be to summon your heart's desire... even if you can't sing.

How do I know *The Magic of Music* is real?

Because I sang the girl of my dreams into my life, simply by harnessing the power of words and music.

Like others, I see musical composition and songwriting as emotional engineering.

Music + Emotion = *How To Attract Your Heart's Desire.*

Whether you have a degree or not, you engineer your life; deciding what to do, when, how, and for how long.

Take your ability to 'engineer' your life via your emotions, and harness the power of creative visualization.

The result?

You will become aware of the connection between the songs you sing and the life you live.

The book you hold in your hands is the product of years of creative experimentation, celebrating glorious words and music in one way or another.

I hope you enjoy *The Magic of Music.*

Oliver Luke Delorie

Music is the universal language of mankind.

Henry Wadsworth Longfellow

MUSIC

Where to begin? The Paleolithic Era of course.

Era is an anagram of ear, but that's beside the point.

When humans first band-ed together :) they poked holes in bones and played them like flutes.

Music is an art form, made up of sound and silence.

The word "music" means "art of the muses" in Greek, and as a musician (or lover of music) you are celebrating the finest art form in existence, the food of muses; the essence of existence.

But's that just my opinion.

Still, there's no doubt any other art form comes as close to stirring the soul as music does (and at a speed of 345 meters per second). Wow.

Certain sounds trigger different (un)conscious responses, like hearing your own name, or a creak in the floorboards late at night when you're all alone.

Elvis Costello said writing about music is about as silly as dancing about architecture.

I see his point, though in my opinion, words continually fail any joyful, profound, deeply meaningful, creative or spiritual activity (such as celebrating the divine with the song in your heart).

The more you play,
the more the
magic spreads.

Maynard James Keenan

MAGIC

Magic is central not only in 'primitive' society, but in 'modern' society as well.

Magic is an attempt to influence, experience and understand the world via language, actions and symbolism. And not surprisingly, most magicians see magic as a practice of spiritual growth.

Though whatever your intentions, the more conscious intention you give to your everyday thoughts, words and actions, the more you will notice the results inevitably showing up in your life.

Apparently, deep down, we humans believe (or remember) our ability to influence the world around us with simple words, whether spoken or not.

But intentional (or magical) language is different from everyday communication because it accesses your emotions by converting your words into symbols.

In other words, unintentional (or un-magical) ordinarily-expressed words simply describe (and conjure) your external, objective reality.

The language of magic (or music for that matter) is intended for a completely different purpose, and is thus why many consider the practice of magic to be sacred.

Magic is the manipulation of words, ideas, images and symbols to change consciousness, so tread lightly.

Music and words
together can be a
powerful thing.

Bryan Ferry

MATH

Some people (theorists, mostly) use math to understand music. And though music has no foundation in mathematics, nature is mathematical, and so is music.

While the Chinese, Egyptians and Mesopotamians studied the mathematics of sound, Pythagoreans in Greece were the first to look deeper, where they found that musical scales fit neatly into numerical ratios.

Their main conclusion at the time was that "all nature consists of harmony arising out of numbers."

Strings vibrate at numerically-charted frequencies, and sound waves are understood with math equations.

Cellos, for instance, are built with numerical formulas to resonate in a desired way.

But music theory is not just for composers, singers, songwriters, and soon-to-be channels of heart-stuff.

Music is for everyone!

Why are there 12 notes in our musical scale?

Who cares. You don't have to know how music works to know that it works.

My intention is to encourage you to make your own music (and therefore magic) so you can not only enjoy the celebration of creating your life with joyful sonic intention, but also reap the rewards that come with conscious co-creation.

Music keeps me alive.

Miley Cyrus

VIBRATION

Everything has its own vibration (as if it were emitting a radio signal) so all we need to do is 'dial in' our heart's desire.

Music can immediately shift your vibration up or down (and however quickly you want to make the shift).

If you're set to 95.3, you can only hear / see / feel nouns vibrating at that same frequency.

So if you want to attract something vibrating at 100.3, you have to tune yourself to 100.3!

It's that simple.

It doesn't matter who or what you wish to attract, this is the basis behind *The Magic of Music*.

Don't believe it?

This is so simple, it should be blowing your mind!

It's not called magic for nothing.

Finally, your life won't budge an inch unless you push your limits.

So crank that dial up to 100.3!

If this ain't clicking for you, there's no reason to read any further.

Put this book down now and go do something else.

Music is to the soul
what words are
to the mind.

Modest Mouse

INCANTATION

A spell or charm made up of words is called an incantation, its roots in the Latin word *incantare* meaning "to sing a spell".

Sure, it's witchcraft, but everybody's doing it (to some degree or another) whether they know it or not.

A chant, also called a rune, is most powerful when it's simple and repetitive. This is important; remember this.

Every song you sing is an incantation, and the tone, vibe and thoughts behind the words and the meaning all have an effect on your mood. Sing a sad song over and over and over again and see how you feel.

A spell consists of a verse, formula, or set or words, ritual actions, or any of the above.

But forget the structure. Just use the symbols, words and ideas that fcel right to you.

When you are busy summoning your heart's desire, you are literally calling upon the universal heart (or equivalent) to help you meet your desire face-to-face.

All religions use prayers, liturgies, singing and chanting to invoke feelings of connection to source.

Again, everybody's doing it (whether they know it or not).

For those eager to make the connection, the secular alternative to a prayer is an affirmation.

Both sexes endeavor
to charm each other with
musical notes and rhythm.

Charles Darwin

ATTRACTION

If you're reading this book, you probably have some understanding of (or at least an interest in) the law of attraction.

Music is the fastest way to help you attract what you want, whether or not you are in alignment (vibrational harmony) with what makes most sustainable (natural) sense to you, your lifestyle and your dreams.

Everything in existence has electrical current running through it, which is why everything is actually *alive.*

When you let (or allow) your heart's desire into your life, attraction is at work.

This is when he / she / it shows up, and how / why you are able to ultimately connect with him / her / it.

Conscious awareness of this powerful force will allow you to focus your energy, time, effort and attention on vibrating / harmonizing / aligning with your desire(s).

Make sense?

You are attracting and repelling verbs, nouns and adjectives all day long, so doesn't it make sense to keep your finger on the pulse (or to find it in the first place)?

Both blackbirds and starlings use song to attract mates, while whales sing for 24 hours at a time during mating season!

People haven't always
been there for me,
but music always has.

Taylor Swift

EMOTION

How do you feel right now?

Are you listening to music in the background?

What do you think you're attracting into your life this instant, feeling how you're feeling at this moment in time?

Music activates and triggers emotional responses, so when your emotions are heightened, you are more susceptible to suggestion.

So: what un- or sub-conscious 'suggestions' are you sending out into the ethers?

Let's look at what is known as your *Emotional Guidance System.*

Your emotional guidance system follows the same principle as every other trick up the sleeve of this book.

Like attracts like, so when using your emotions as a guide as to whether or not you're summoning your heart's desire, ask yourself: *how do I feel?*

Are your feelings attracting or repelling him / her / it?

Emotions are the name of the game. They are why and how *The Magic of Music* works in the first place.

Or at all, for that matter.

Music has healing power.

Elton John

RHYTHM

Bop along with the turn signal in your car.

Hum along with the tone of the vacuum cleaner.

You have rhythm inside you, even if you don't believe it.

Your body ticks like a clock. Tick tock tick tock. Use your natural groove to make your dreams come true.

Whether you understand the patterns allowing you to feel the music deep down in your soul (or not) you have to agree: you are affected on the most subtle levels by the groove of your favorite music.

Dictionaries define groove as an enjoyable rhythm that makes people who can't dance want to.

Groove is what makes your inner music breathe.

When you're in the flow, it's not about what you are singing / playing, but *how* you are singing / playing it.

Are you feeling it?

You don't need talent. If you have a pulse, you can do this.

Tap your toes to your own, unique magical song until you can taste your dreams.

Match the groove of your thoughts with what you're passionate about. It works.

Music can sooth
a savage beast, soften rocks,
or bend a knotted oak.

Will Congreve

RHYME

What sounds good to you?

Whatever you like, chances are the lyrics or words rhyme, employing the sexy symmetry of set patterns.

Rhymes are mnemonic, which means they help you remember and learn [insert subject here].

What are you repeating to yourself over and over?

What verses and choruses are you singing over and over again in the shower or in the car?

How did you learn them so easily?

Sweet-sounding rhyme.

Your ears, brain and body crave the expectation of rhyme, thanks to the fact they are simple, pleasant and easy to understand.

Rhymes are verbal intelligence. They both relax and stimulate your mind. So use this lovely literary device to enhance the effectiveness of your 'spells'.

I have said for years *The Magic of Music* is based on rhythm and rhyme, so be sure to build your heart's foundation on these two essential elements.

Charm your desire with rhyme's fire.

First food, then clothes,
then shelter, then music.

Christian Nestell Bovee

REPETITION

Repeat after me.

Now pick a melody or rhythm you like and repeat it.

Repeating something you like over and over again not only reinforces the good feelings of 'liking it' but also works to unify your 'song'.

Theorists (again) believe that music is based on repetition, so repetition of your favorite hooks, lyrics or melodies remind you of past emotional states.

Every time you hear notes / songs / music / tunes / beats, the emotional centers in your brain are activated.

A stuffy German once said "repetition and popular music is psychotic and infantile" whereas saner views suggest that music is enjoyed by more people when it is inclusive (pop), rather than exclusive (jazz).

It's likely that you can relate to the simple, common denominators in pop music more often than you can enjoy (let alone sit through) brainy noodling and numerous, complicated chord and key changes.

A great way to train your musical ear and learn pitch is to get a banjo, hurdy-gurdy, shruti box, didgeridoo or set of bagpipes, and start playing them.

Let the drone of your new toy hypnotize you and put you into a trance that's ripe for manifesting.

Music is said to be
the speech of angels.

Thomas Carlyle

TRANCE

I will count to three, and snap my fingers.

When you are in any state of awareness outside of your normal waking consciousness, you are in a trance.

Wikipedia associates trance with hypnosis and mediation (understandably) which suits our purposes.

Here are some examples of trance states:

- Astral travel
- Deep sleep
- Driving
- (the state of) Ecstasy
- Possession
- Relaxation
- Visualization

When you're in a trance, your brain (and therefore your mind) receive, filter, order and perceive stimuli differently than when you're in normal waking consciousness (obviously).

Professionals and practitioners alike suggest that when you're in a trance, your mind is like a programmable computer, so take advantage of your fertile garden!

A trance is an intense focus of your attention, whether you are consciously focusing on something (or not).

Inducing trance in yourself is easy, especially when you use repetition to repeat sounds, phrases, images, notes, tones, words, feelings or ideas.

Music in the soul
can be heard by
the universe.

Lao Tzu

HYPNOSIS

Who is in control?

You are.

Or are you?

If you remember to notice, you will catch yourself on autopilot, like when you're driving or watching Youtube.

You put yourself into light trance all the time.

Heck, even sleeping or dreaming could be interpreted as hypnosis (especially when you are determined to make deliberate choices in these states).

Daydreaming is a form of hypnosis too. Why not focus your energy and attention on attracting your heart's desire when you're super-relaxed or super-focused?

I understand hypnosis as a state of mind (or frequency of brain waves) that when allowed free rein, allow you to access a deeper (or higher) part of yourself to learn quicker, practice a special skill in your imagination, or remember something important that would usually take longer (or be harder) because of all the distractions.

Hypnotizing (or consciously relaxing) yourself is a way to access a quieter, slower (faster?) way of thinking, so you can sharpen your focus when it comes to attracting your heart's desire.

Woo-hoo!

Music,
to create harmony,
must investigate discord.

Plutarch

MEDITATION

When you are meditating you are distracting yourself.

You train your mind to calm down and let go of (or ignore) the distractions around you, so you can concentrate on breathing, visualizing, intentional day dreaming, etc.

Meditation promotes relaxation, so you can better function in your life, regardless of what you're into.

There are a million ways to mediate; there is no right or wrong way. You have to find what works best for you.

I find one of the simplest ways to meditate is to focus on your breathing. Hear / feel / notice your breath.

In and out. In and out.

Let every other thought you have just come and go. Keep breathing in and out. In and out.

And when you notice you've been distracted (you will), simply start focusing on your breathing again. That's all.

It will take a while (maybe weeks or even months) but if you continue to practice, you will master it. Pow!

Do anything for 10,000 hours and you are a pro.

When you can meditate without distraction, you will have *The Magic of Music* (or any other form of intentional manifesting) at your beck and call.

Music is the art
of the prophets.

Martin Luther

IMAGINATION

Einstein said that imagination is more important than knowledge.

Why would he say such a thing?

Because he knew things few others did.

Knowledge floats around down here on earth, while imagination is universal, stretching to the stars and beyond.

We get knowledge (taught and learned) from our imaginations (and the imaginations of others).

Imagination is the source of all things, known and unknown. Either we imagined it, or someone else did.

Imagination is limitless, unbound by rules, free.

Dream anything you wish; nothing's stopping you.

It doesn't matter who or what turns you on.

Imagine to your heart's content, because attracting your heart's desire will make you content.

There is no doubt, and no limit.

Imagination goes beyond the 5 senses (which is why it's sometimes referred to as the 6th sense).

So follow yours.

Wherever it wants to go.

Music is the
most magical form of
communication there is.

Lesley Garrett

SIMPLICITY

What is easy?

However you wish to woo your heart's desire, keep it simple sweetheart.

The simpler your song, the easier it will be for your brain and body (and therefore the universe / god / source) to manifest him / her / it for you.

When outlining this book, I deliberately chose to keep the ideas and language simple (there's a method to my musical madness).

Especially with your short attention span (you're not alone) the easier, simpler and quicker the entire process, the faster you will see results.

Sure, you can make it complex, but don't be discouraged by thinking or feeling like you need to compose a symphony-length tune when all you want to do is feel good while calling forth your heart's desire.

It's easy to make things complicated.

What takes real skill and street smarts is to keep things simple.

Why make something complicated when it doesn't have to be?

You will get further faster if you remember to keep your songs down to a few syllables, notes, words or less.

Music has the power
to bring people
together.

Edgar Winter

OPPOSITES

Nothing can exist without its opposite.

Opposites exist everywhere, in everything. No exceptions.

The more you think you want something, the less it will make you happy (hopefully you know this already).

You may have also noticed that what you want never truly fulfills your needs. That's because wants can never be sustainably satisfied. Wants are insatiable.

Getting your needs fulfilled, on the other hand, is a little easier. When your needs are fulfilled, you find inner peace, security, safety, comfort and / or calm.

I want to remind you of opposites for one reason:

Do not be surprised when your heart's desire doesn't show up post-haste.

Sometimes we think our wants are our heart's desire, when in fact, our needs are our heart's desire. And then fears and worries wrench their way in there just to mess it all up (it happens to everyone).

You can easily get caught up in chasing, striving and struggling for a firm grip on your wants, yet if you take a step back and reflect on your results, you will surely find your true needs (your heart's desires) have been met and fulfilled many times over.

Just sayin'.

A musician must make
music, an artist must paint,
and a poet must write,
if they are to be ultimately
at peace with themselves.

Abraham Maslow

HEALING

You can heal your life with sound.

Of course, if you don't believe me, then you can't.

As you're learning, *The Magic of Music* is all about summoning your heart's desire by harnessing the super sonic power of the universe.

If you can sing any person, place, thing or experience to you, surely you can at least aid in the healing process, regardless of what ailment is ailing you.

Sing along with Sinead O'Connor:

Thank you for healing me
Thank you for healing me
Thank you for healing me
Thank you for healing me

Give it some sort of beat and some sort of groove or feeling, and even a note (note is an anagram of tone).

Sing or hum or whistle this over and over and over again, as often as you remember to, and you will likely see your tumor shrink, your skin heal, or your hair grow back.

If you believe self-healing is possible, *The Magic of Music* can help you heal yourself.

If radiant health is your heart's desire, sing it into existence by aligning yourself with the pulse of all life.

Music is my religion.

Jimi Hendrix

POWER

What created you and everything you know?

Where did everything come from?

I'll tell you.

Everything is made of light and sound.

Yes, everything is made up of varying quantities of light and sound.

Sound is one-half of creation. One half of everything.

The power of music (harnessed, channeled, finely-tuned intentioned sound) is so (un)believably incredible, you must practice it for maximum effect.

There's a reason music is so popular. It's powerful. Music can control you, your body and your emotions (without you even knowing what's happening).

How wonderful is that?

Sing / say this over and over again:

I am powerful
I am powerful
I am powerful
I am powerful

Watch / witch what happens.

I want to hypnotize
my fans so when they
hear my music they
love themselves
instantly.

Lady Gaga

DESIRE

What turns you on?

What brings you joy?

What makes you laugh?

What makes you cry?

What makes you do both at the same time?

I love these questions so much, I ask them often.

I ask these questions so you won't get mixed up and distracted and dissuaded by glittering gold, marvelous money and seductive stuff.

Yes, fame and fortune are a good time, but when you chase desire you are chasing a carrot on a stick. You may get a bite, but then a bigger carrot shows up, and the game goes on. And on. And on.

Desire is high octane fuel, no doubt.

Use it wisely for your heart-felt purposes, and you will see double the results from your efforts than you would have otherwise.

Music inspires desire, but before you go for it, ask yourselff:

What are you really after?

And remember: *Thou shalt not covet* [fill in the blank].

Sweeping the floor
or brushing your hair
can be turned into a spell.

Teresa Moorey

SING

Even if you can't.

Sure, you may like or dislike your voice, but your own interpretation is what makes your voice (however you choose to express it) unique.

And therefore special.

Heck, even if you can't sing (e.g. think you can't hold a note) it doesn't matter.

Your voice can be accompanied or not, rhyme (or not), repeat itself (or not).

There are no rules!

Human beings have been singing for thousands of years (even if they were 'off key'), while birds, whales, insects, rodents and canines all sing songs to identify themselves, protect themselves and attract mates.

Mimic a sound you hear (you are rarely surrounded in silence).

Sure, you'll be more comfortable when you're alone, so make some space for yourself to experiment and play around.

Make it fun, because the more you enjoy expressing yourself, the easier (and quicker) manifesting your heart's desire will be!

And then he / she / it will appear.

Out of thin air.

What do you call
a musician with a
college degree?

~

Night manager
at McDonalds.

DANCE

Exercise gets you naturally high and happy (and we learn by literally being flexible) so move!

We integrate our sensory system with our motor system, which means adding (any) physical sensation to our attraction process helps us get into the groove.

And (you might have also guessed) you can also attract your heart's desire even if you can't dance!

If you aren't having as much success as you'd like, physical activity may be the missing ingredient, because the more you feel the music, the more powerful your intentions / chants / rhymes / prayers will be.

Are you digging it?

When you feel *anything*, you're sending a message out into the ethers like a radio signal, that will either draw your heart's desire to you, or push it away.

So tap your toes or bob your head along with the music you love.

There's a reason dance has always been celebrated so passionately in every country and culture in the world.

Dance is danced because it feels good.

Now you have another ingredient in your recipe.

The only truth is music.

Jack Kerouac

STYLE

From the whisper of the wind to death rap / metal, there are about as many style of music as there are 'musicians' on earth.

That being said, feel free to develop your own style.

For one, there are no rules, so don't impose any upon yourself, or your dreams or your goals.

If you like death metal, rock on!

If you like little more than the whisper of the wind, sway along with this subtle yet powerful phenomenon.

You have already (unconsciously) emotionally engineered your life based on your musical tastes, so why stop now?

The music you make can move mountains.

Let your favorite music inspire you to create the life you want.

Like sympathetic strings (on a sitar for example) as you sing your song, similarly-tuned people, places and things start vibrating along with you, harmonizing with you as you (again) engineer your life.

There are 7 billion ways to do everything; 7 billion styles if you will (that means you're free to experiment in any way, shape or form that feels good to you).

The point is to express yourself (even if you think you can't) like the saying *dance like no one is watching.*

Music can name
the unnameable
and communicate
the unknowable.

Leonard Bernstein

BELIEF

Believe in your fears and they will always be there.

But sing them away, and they won't hold nearly as much power over you.

When you are singing / drumming / playing / humming / imagining / pretending / dancing / chanting / visualizing or practicing, you are creating your reality.

You will continue to see your beliefs manifested in your life as long as you keep them bottled up inside you (because there's no where else for them to go).

All they can do is come out.

They don't have a choice!

Whenever you find yourself practicing *The Magic of Music,* you are unearthing your heart's desire... but only if you believe it with all your heart.

That's why it's called your heart's desire. If you really want it, you need to believe in your heart that it's possible.

In fact, this is the only obstacle to celebrating your life while you're still alive here on earth.

Get to the bottom of what you believe.

How? Take a look around.

You will see evidence of what you believe everywhere you look.

What's the difference
between a banjo
and an onion?

~

Nobody cries when
you chop up a banjo.

SENSES

Most people limit their powers of attracting to seeing or visualizing their wildest dreams.

But, as you know, you have more than 5 senses at your disposal. They are:

- Sight
- Hearing
- Touch
- Taste
- Smell
- Intuition

Because most people are ignoring (or simply not harnessing) the power of their other senses, they are not getting the best bang for their buck. It's like reading one page of a book; you get a feel for the subject, but you're not getting the big picture.

So when you can't imagine the details (taste, smell, feeling) of what you desire, try using props, rituals or images to help you. This is incredibly effective.

William Fezler says that to make something real, you need to experience it with all 5 senses (duh).

Start slowly.

Enjoy the learning curve.

Stimulate your senses (especially the ones you haven't exercised in a while). Like toys, I'm sure senses collect dust if not taken out of the box and played with once in a while.

Music can give us strength
when we are weak,
sight when we are blind,
and ears when we are deaf.

Zarine Narielvala

CHAKRAS

For those so inclined, I just couldn't keep this out of the book. It's too much fun to ponder and great food for thought.

Chakra	Vowel	Tone	Frequency	Color	Sense
Crown	Ee (wheel)	B	480 Hz	Indigo	None
Third Eye	Ih (interest)	A	426.7 Hz	Violet	Intuition
Throat	Eh (weather)	G	384.7 Hz	Blue	Hearing
Heart	Ah (family)	F	341.3 Hz	Green	Touch
Solar Plexus	Aw (awe)	E	320 Hz	Yellow	Sight
Belly	Oh (smoke)	D	288 Hz	Orange	Taste
Root	Oo (smooth)	C	256 Hz	Red	Smell

(From *Sounding The Inner Landscape* by Kay Gardner)

Kay suggests visualizing the corresponding color to the sound / chakra you are focusing on, all while remembering to breathe, of course.

Author's Note: I have yet to take this information and run with it in my own magical music practice, though I imagine if / when you do, you will be unstoppable!

Share this with a musically-inclined friend.

They will love it.

How do you get a
trombonist off
your porch?

~

Pay him for the pizza.

COMMUNICATION

Yoko Ono once said the Key of C was the key of communication. This makes sense to me; the major key is a common denominator.

I see music in the key of C as accessible, easy, simple. And thus able to communicate in a more inclusive way.

Speaking of communication, we often think of words. And because this is a book about magic (filled with words) what's the magic word?

Here are some other famous words and phrases (to remind you how silly you can make all of this):

- Abracadabra
- Alakazam
- By the Power of Greyskull
- Bippity boppity boop
- Hocus pocus
- Mecca lecca hi mecca hiney ho
- Open sesame
- Presto chango
- Shazam!

Craig Conley says this sort of non-sensical language is still an instrument of creation, though "calling something by its true name gives you an edge" say the Wiccans.

In some circles, magical language, chants, spells or incantations are kept secret.

So keep yours secret if you like; it can't hurt.

Music touches us emotionally, where words alone can't.

Johnny Depp

UNIVERSALITY

No matter the culture, everyone is on earth practices *The Magic of Music* in one way or another.

Lutheran litany is repetitive praying, or a series of invocations, while the Council of Vaison in 529 decreed "Let that beautiful and sweet chant custom be maintained and continued day and night without interruption, as it could never produce disgust or weariness."

Mantras may not make sense to untrained ears, but Hindus, Buddhists and Sikhs have been expressing themselves with sacred sounds for 3000 years, using syllables or words believed to have spiritual power.

They are mathematically structured, melodic, and full of longing for truth, reality, peace and love.

In Chinese, the word mantra means "true words" (some people believe mantras are older than language).

And knights used to recite a prayer called a lorica to protect them before going into battle.

In African-American folk spirituality, hoodoo (or folk magic) hymns are sung in praise or adoration of a deity, all with the aim to access supernatural forces for help.

Again, there are are 7 billion ways to do everything (which means there are 7 billion songs to be sung).

What will you sing into being?

What will you never say
about a mandolin player?
~
That's the mandolin
player's Porsche.

AFFIRMATIONS

Two of my professional heros Tony Robbins and Brendan Burchard shout their affirmations from their stages with emotion, intensity and conviction.

However you like to affirm your beliefs (new or tried and true) the more emotion, feeling, passion and confidence you infuse them with, the better.

Are you starting to see a pattern?

To clarify: an affirmation (like a mantra or pop song) is a saying, prayer, hymn, chant, idea, string of words, praise or positive statement that affirms something you would like to remember, believe in, or trust.

Like anything you want to learn, the more you drill it into your head, the more you will remember / internalize / ultimately believe it, eventually acting as if it's true.

So in the case of manifesting your heart's desire, the more boomerangs you toss out into the void, the more results you are bound to see.

Agree?

I don't mind repeating it: there are no rules.

Make up your own affirmations based on your own hopes and dreams, and start focusing on what you want (instead of worrying about what you fear).

What's the difference
between a chicken
on the road, and a
musician on the road?

~

There's a remote chance
the chicken is on
its way to a gig.

CONCLUSION

Again, no one has ever been able to put their finger on the collective pulse and come to a consensus on what music is, so (again) you're free to express yourself any way you like.

I made up a simple song under a full moon one night wandering the streets of my neighborhood, trying to avoid my friends who were partying and keeping me up.

I remember *knowing* that I was manipulating the world around me (like when Neo finally saw for himself the neon green energy pattern of symbols and numbers at the end of The Matrix).

This is all I said:

It's easy
She loves me
I have money

I'm healthy
I'm happy
I'm lucky

Over and over and over again, every day for weeks.

Whenever I said (or sang) it, I gave my personal rhyme a simple tempo, and an even simpler tune.

Yes, it took a few months to work, but I was patient.

Again, I *knew* I was calling [her] to me.

So I did.

Love is a friendship
set to music.

Joseph Campbell

QUESTIONS & ANSWERS

How do I know what my deepest desires are?

What do you seek / covet / desire more than anything?
The answer to this question is your deepest desire.

What is the difference between wants and needs?

Wants are passing pleasures. Needs are joyfully sustainable lasting treasures.

How do I know if [my deepest desire] is what I want?

There is only one way to find out.

How do I know if [my deepest desire] is what I need?

You will know the answer when you stop trying to fulfill your endless, insatiable wants.

How can music help me?

Music is the finest art form there is. How could anything this cool NOT help you?

How can magic help me?

Every single person on earth is using magic to create their lives, in one form or another. What have you got to lose?

What is rhythm and why is it so awesome?

Without the steady metronome of your heart, you would die.

What's the difference between a musician and a Mutual Fund?

~

One will eventually mature and make some money.

What is rhyme and why is it so awesome?

Rhyme sounds good.

What is repetition and why is it so awesome?

Repetition makes the world go round.

Is it truly possible to summon my deepest desire?

You tell me. Either way you're right.

Can anyone summon their deepest desire?

You are doing it whether you know it / like it or not.

How can I stay on track and remember to practice?

What's more important: re-runs of reality TV or your ultimate happiness?

What do I do once I get what I thought I wanted?

Enjoy it and let it go if / when it wants. You don't have a choice.

How can I help others summon their deepest desires?

Realize how fun it is to give instead of get.

Is magic the work of the devil?

Yep. You're evil and you're going to hell. See you there!

Is music the work of the devil?

Yes. That's why it's so awesome. Just kidding, scaredy cat :)

I think music
is the greatest art
form that exists.

Eddie Vedder

What if it doesn't work at first?

"If at first you don't succeed, try try again", remember?

What if I can't sing or clap or whistle or hum?

Then you got a bad attitude.

What if I don't even like music?

Then I pity your sad, sorry soul.

What if I have no imagination?

You're not alone. Many people use their other senses to daydream nouns into their lives.

What if I don't know how to write?

You can talk, right?

What if I have no feelings?

Then you're a robot. Find someone to reprogram you.

What if I'm tone deaf?

Acceptance is a virtue.

What if I think I'm too old or too young?

Grow up or give up.

What if my friends or family think I'm weird?

They already think you're weird. Get over it.

Ah, music. A magic
beyond all we do here!

J.K. Rowling

What if I've failed at everything I've ever tried?

It's never to late to live the life you have always imagined.

Why am I supposed to believe any of this?

You believed it enough to buy or borrow this book in the first place!

What makes you the expert?

Singing simple rhymes over and over again in a state of deep relaxation brought me my heart's desire.

Without music,
life would
be a mistake.

Friedrich Nietzsche

INTERVIEW

Who or what inspired you to play music?

Listening to John Frusciante inspired me to start playing guitar. Then one day in high school, I was happily annoying everyone on the bus with my kazoo cacaphony when my friend Natalie gave me a drum and said "play this instead". I've never looked back.

What inspires you now?

Playing the piano. Programming electronic music. It's all creative energy; it just takes different forms as I change, and as the people, places and world change around me.

Why did you write The Magic of Music?

I wrote The Magic of Music for two reasons. The first reason was to gather and record my ideas to teach myself something new. That's why I study and travel and read and ask questions. The other reason I wrote the book was to share what I've learned on my journey, regarding the incredible power of music.

Did you sing your other books into existence too?

Everything in existence begins with a thought, which proves that anything we want to create starts out as invisible-to-the-eye quantum bits of seeming nothingness. So to answer that question, the answer is yes, I do imagine all my books and music, I suppose 'channeling' them as I go. The best part is: this is nothing new. You can do it too.

If music be the food
of love, play on!

William Shakespeare

How do you define success?

I get bugged when I can't seem to think for myself. I'm so brainwashed to chase awards and recognition and fame and fortune from sharing my creative work. That being said, I define success as being able to spend my time as I want. I used to define success as sleeping in, but now it's experiencing joy.

What style of music inspires you?

Any form of music without words. Classical, instrumental, electronic, or music in other languages where I don't know what they're saying (laughs).

What's your passion?

In a nutshell, my passion is composing, recording and performing inspirational music, and writing and publishing books. If I have a mission, I believe I am on earth to empower creatives of all ages.

Why do you value creative expression so much?

I value creative expression because it's the only thing that saved me from losing hope. When I'm writing a song, or working on a book, or editing, or composing, or recording, or performing, I feel possessed by a power greater than myself. I am amazed at how I can even play piano. I hold creative self-expression in high regard because the ideas, feelings and visions I get when I'm being creative both comfort and terrify me. I'm always learning. Especially when I just get out of the way and press record or start doodling.

If I were not a physicist,
I would probably be
a musician.

Albert Einstein

How has music changed your life?

Playing music gave me the confidence I needed, when I needed it most. The ability to express my emotions is inexplicably comforting to me. I feel lucky to hear the voice of my soul reflected back to me either in my headphones, on the speakers, or in the movement of the audience when they're dancing their hearts out.

What matters most to you?

Feeling joy. Expressing sadness. Sharing passion with kindred spirits. Laughing at my mistakes. Singing, dancing and drumming myself into a trance. That's the best. Nothing I love more than drumming.

What instrument would like to be able to play?

If I had the patience, I would learn how to play the fiddle. Yep. I must have been Irish in a past life.

What would you say to your 10-year-old self?

That's a good one (pause). I would tell him the path would get rocky and bumpy like he can't yet imagine. I would tell him to start expressing himself with art, music, writing. I would tell him to find a way to connect to the source of creation, so he would be better able to navigate the inevitable storms that will rage around him. I would also tell him that he can always trust his creative spark. Even if no one else seems to value it, it is pure gold. I like to say "if you speak from the heart, you can't go wrong" so that's how I would speak to him.

Some people have lives;
some people have music.

John Green

GRATITUDE

I would like to publicly appreciate the following peeps:

The Ivanys
The Lundmarks
The Levins
The Cooks
The Lidells
The Meiers
The Dedovics
Rev. Michael Beckwith
Rev. Dale Jukes
Angela Ortega
Jill Banting
Robin Crow
Antonia Partridge
Jeff Emmett
Darrin Caruso
Tanya Pauls
Cindy Lee Yelland
Kimberly Davitsky
Nyree Marsh
Richelle Boutaud
Kelly Gee
Cynthia Mac
Angela Roy
John Fraser
Dr. John DeMartini
Michael Losier
Ernie Zelinksi
Andrew Kelly
Jana Stanfield
Wayne Dyer
Dexter Newton
Anita Rehker

Life, he realized,
was much like a song.

Nicholas Sparks

BIBLIOGRAPHY

Music and Mathematics
Thomas M. Fiore

The Twelve-Tone Musical Scale
Keith Enevoldsen

The Complete Idiot's Guide To Music Theory
Michael Miller

This Is Your Brain on Music
Daniel J. Levitin

Sounding The Inner Landscape
Kay Gardner

Creating The Groove
Stews Lessons

Witchcraft, A Beginner's Guide
Teresa Moorey

Law of Attraction
Michael Losier

The Teachings of Abraham
Esther & Jerry Hicks

The Magical Power of Words
S.J. Tambiah

After silence, that which
comes nearest to expressing
the inexpressible is music.

Aldous Huxley

WHAT DO YOU WANT?

_____

_____

_____

_____

_____

_____

_____

_____

_____

_____

_____

_____

Where words leave off,
music begins.

Heinrich Heine

MAKE IT RHYME

_____

_____

_____

_____

_____

_____

_____

_____

_____

_____

_____

Tell me what you listen
to, and I'll tell you
who you are.

Tiffanie DeBartolo

MAKE IT REAL

_____

_____

_____

_____

_____

_____

_____

_____

_____

_____

_____

_____

Do you feel your music?

Michael Jackson

WHAT'S NEXT ON YOUR LIST?

www.ingramcontent.com/pod-product-compliance
Lightning Source LLC
Chambersburg PA
CBHW071057040426
42443CB00013B/3364